The Gingerbread Golem's Culinary Alchemy

The Gingerbread Golem's Culinary Alchemy

Matthew Petchinsky

The Gingerbread Golem's Culinary Alchemy: Enchanting Recipes for a Sweetly Dark Feast
By: Matthew Petchinsky

Introduction: The Legend of the Gingerbread Golem: A Culinary Tale of Magic and Flavor

In the frosty depths of winter, as the world wraps itself in the crystalline embrace of snow and ice, a peculiar tale has traveled down the winding corridors of time—an enchanting legend whispered by hearth-fires and woven into the very fabric of holiday traditions. The story of the Gingerbread Golem is not merely one of confectionary delight; it is a saga of magic, creativity, and the enduring bond between myth and culinary artistry.

The Origins of the Gingerbread Golem

According to folklore, the Gingerbread Golem was born in a time when harsh winters often meant scarcity and struggle. In a humble village surrounded by dense, frostbitten woods, a wise baker, known both for her exquisite gingerbread and her mystical touch, sought to protect her community from the icy perils of the season. Legends tell that this baker, drawing upon ancient alchemical practices and a deep love for her people, crafted the first Gingerbread Golem.

Using the sacred spices of the season—ginger for warmth, cinnamon for protection, and cloves for strength—she infused her dough with not only flavor but intent. She shaped the dough into a grand figure, decorating it with sugared icicles and frosting runes meant to ward off evil and invoke abundance. Then, with the light of the solstice moon shining through her workshop window, she whispered an incantation as the Golem baked. When it emerged from the oven, the figure was no mere confection; it stood tall, ready to shield her village from harm.

A Protector and a Feast

The Gingerbread Golem was said to have guarded the village through the bitter season, patrolling the frosty streets, ensuring homes stayed safe from wolves and the bone-chilling winds. But the golem's purpose was twofold. Once the winter softened and the earth began its thaw, the villagers gathered to celebrate their survival. In an act of gratitude and reverence, they deconstructed the Gingerbread Golem, feasting on its pieces to imbibe the protective magic and celebrate the return of prosperity.

This act of consuming the golem was not a mere indulgence but a symbolic ritual. The villagers believed that by partaking of the golem's body, they absorbed the blessings and strength it embodied, ensuring health, wealth, and unity for the year to come.

The Evolution of the Legend

Over centuries, the tale of the Gingerbread Golem evolved, adapting to the cultures and kitchens that embraced it. Some regions reimagined the golem as a mischievous guardian, playfully rearranging holiday decorations or sneaking bits of candy from children's stockings. Others viewed it as a wise mentor, offering guidance through cryptic messages revealed in frosting patterns.

As culinary arts advanced, so too did the artistry of the Gingerbread Golem. Intricate designs and innovative techniques transformed it from a simple protector into a festive masterpiece. Yet, at its core, the golem remained a symbol of resilience, creativity, and the enduring magic of human ingenuity.

The Magical Essence of Gingerbread

What makes gingerbread so uniquely suited to this legend? The spices—ginger, cinnamon, nutmeg, and cloves—are not only flavorful but imbued with centuries-old symbolic meanings. Ginger is said to warm the spirit and ignite creativity, while cinnamon offers protection and healing. Nutmeg is linked to prosperity and clarity, and cloves are thought to repel negativity. Together, these spices create a sensory experience that transcends mere taste, evoking a sense of comfort, warmth, and enchantment.

When combined with honey, molasses, or sugar, these spices create a sweet alchemy that binds people across time and culture. The very act of crafting gingerbread—mixing, rolling, shaping, and decorating—is a meditative practice, a way of channeling intention into creation.

A Culinary Journey Awaits

In this cookbook, we honor the legacy of the Gingerbread Golem by blending tradition with innovation. These recipes are not just about baking; they are about crafting stories, creating memories, and embracing the magic that lives in every bite. From the basics of constructing a gingerbread figure to the intricate details of edible enchantments, each chapter invites you to step into the role of baker and alchemist.

As you explore these recipes, remember that every piece of gingerbread you create carries with it a spark of the Gingerbread Golem's magic—a reminder of protection, celebration, and the sweetness of community. Whether you're building an edible fortress or stirring a spiced elixir, let your imagination and intention guide you. The Gingerbread Golem awaits in your kitchen, ready to inspire, protect, and delight.

Welcome to the world of culinary alchemy. Let the magic begin!

Chapter 1: Building the Foundation – Gingerbread Basics

The journey to crafting a Gingerbread Golem begins with a sturdy and flavorful foundation: the dough. A perfectly prepared gingerbread dough is not just about taste; it must have the right texture and structural integrity to support intricate designs and decorations. In this chapter, we will explore every element of creating the ultimate gingerbread dough, from selecting ingredients to ensuring the dough is strong enough for complex builds while still remaining delicious.

Understanding the Essentials: Ingredients Matter

To craft a gingerbread dough worthy of a golem, you need to understand the role of each ingredient. The right balance of flavor, structure, and pliability comes from these core components:

- **Flour (All-Purpose or Bread Flour):** The backbone of your dough, providing structure. Bread flour, with its higher protein content, is ideal for architectural builds due to its strength, while all-purpose flour can work for softer, more edible designs.
- **Molasses:** This ingredient not only deepens the flavor but also gives gingerbread its signature dark color. Unsulfured molasses is preferred for its balanced taste and lack of bitterness.
- **Spices:** The heart of gingerbread lies in its warming spices. Use fresh ginger for a punchy heat, ground cinnamon for warmth, cloves for depth, and nutmeg for a subtle earthiness. You can customize the spice blend to suit your preferences.
- **Sugar:** A mix of brown sugar (for moisture and flavor) and granulated sugar ensures the right level of sweetness and crispness.
- **Fat (Butter or Shortening):** Butter adds richness and a tender crumb, while shortening provides a more neutral flavor and extra stability for structural pieces.
- **Leavening Agents (Baking Soda or Powder):** These help the dough rise slightly during baking, creating a smooth surface. For large builds, use less leavening to minimize puffing and distortion.

- **Eggs:** Eggs act as a binder, holding everything together. For a vegan option, a flaxseed egg substitute works well.
- **Liquid (Milk or Water):** A small amount of liquid ensures the dough holds its shape without being too sticky.

The Perfect Gingerbread Dough Recipe

Here's a tried-and-true recipe for creating gingerbread dough suitable for golems, houses, or decorative designs:

Ingredients:

- 6 cups all-purpose flour (or 5 ½ cups bread flour)
- 1 tablespoon ground ginger
- 2 teaspoons ground cinnamon
- 1 teaspoon ground cloves
- ½ teaspoon ground nutmeg
- 1 teaspoon baking soda
- 1 teaspoon salt
- 1 cup unsalted butter, softened
- 1 cup dark brown sugar, packed
- 1 cup unsulfured molasses
- 2 large eggs
- 1 tablespoon vanilla extract

Instructions:

1. **Mix Dry Ingredients:** In a large bowl, whisk together the flour, spices, baking soda, and salt. Set aside.
2. **Cream Butter and Sugar:** In a stand mixer fitted with a paddle attachment, cream the butter and brown sugar on medium speed until light and fluffy (about 2 minutes).
3. **Incorporate Molasses and Eggs:** Reduce speed to low and add the molasses, eggs, and vanilla extract. Mix until fully combined.
4. **Combine Wet and Dry Ingredients:** Gradually add the dry ingredients to the wet mixture, mixing on low speed. Stop once the dough starts to come together—overmixing can make it tough.

5. **Chill the Dough:** Divide the dough into two discs, wrap in plastic wrap, and refrigerate for at least 2 hours or overnight. Chilled dough is easier to handle and retains its shape during baking.

Techniques for Rolling and Cutting

Once your dough is chilled, it's time to shape it into the pieces that will form your Gingerbread Golem or other creations. Here are key tips for rolling and cutting:

1. **Prepare the Workspace:** Lightly flour a clean surface and rolling pin to prevent sticking. For structural pieces, consider rolling dough directly onto parchment paper or silicone mats to avoid distortion during transfer.
2. **Roll Evenly:** Aim for a consistent thickness of about ¼ inch for structural pieces. Thinner dough may break, while thicker pieces might not bake evenly.
3. **Use Templates:** If building a Gingerbread Golem or similar structures, create paper or cardboard templates beforehand. Lay the templates on the dough and use a sharp knife or pastry cutter to cut precise shapes.
4. **Chill Again:** After cutting, place the shapes back into the refrigerator for 15–20 minutes. This step ensures the pieces retain their edges during baking.

Baking for Perfection

Proper baking is essential for strong, long-lasting gingerbread structures. Follow these steps:

1. **Preheat the Oven:** Set your oven to 350°F (175°C). Line baking sheets with parchment paper.
2. **Bake in Batches:** Place the chilled shapes on prepared baking sheets, leaving space between pieces to account for slight expansion.
3. **Monitor Baking Time:** Bake smaller pieces for 8–10 minutes and larger, structural pieces for 12–15 minutes. Keep a close eye during the last few minutes—overbaking can lead to brittleness, while underbaking may result in a lack of rigidity.
4. **Cool Completely:** Allow the pieces to cool on the baking sheets for 5 minutes before transferring to a wire rack. Fully cooled gingerbread is firmer and easier to handle.

Strengthening Structural Components

For large or intricate builds, reinforce your gingerbread pieces using these methods:

- **Edible Glue:** Royal icing made with egg whites or meringue powder creates a strong adhesive for assembling parts.
- **Heat Bonding:** Slightly melt edges of gingerbread pieces and press them together for an additional layer of stability.
- **Hidden Support:** For towering golems or houses, use dowels or candy canes as internal supports.

Troubleshooting Common Issues

- **Cracking Dough:** Add a tablespoon of water at a time to moisten overly dry dough.
- **Warped Shapes:** Roll the dough evenly and ensure thorough chilling before baking.
- **Fragile Pieces:** Bake slightly longer to ensure rigidity but avoid overbrowning.

With the foundational skills of gingerbread dough mastered, you are now ready to embark on the magical journey of crafting your Gingerbread Golem. This chapter equips you with the tools, techniques, and confidence to create a deliciously enchanting masterpiece that not only stands tall but also tells a story with every bite.

Chapter 2: Enchanted Frostings and Edible Paints

The Gingerbread Golem, a mythical guardian and masterpiece of culinary creativity, requires more than just a strong foundation to truly come alive. The secret to transforming your creation into a magical showstopper lies in the intricate details—frostings, icings, and edible paints. These finishing touches not only add beauty and charm but also infuse your golem with a sense of enchantment and personality.

In this chapter, you will learn to master the art of making and using enchanted frostings and edible paints. From vibrant colors to dazzling effects, these techniques will elevate your gingerbread creation from impressive to unforgettable.

The Art of Magical Frosting: Types and Uses

Before diving into recipes, it's important to understand the different types of frostings and their uses:

1. **Royal Icing:**

    Known for its smooth finish and hardening properties, royal icing is the cornerstone of gingerbread decoration. It serves as both an adhesive for structural pieces and a medium for intricate designs.

2. **Buttercream Frosting:**

    Rich and creamy, buttercream is best for decorative accents that won't harden completely. While less sturdy than royal icing, it adds a delicious layer of flavor.

3. **Glaze Icing:**

    Made with powdered sugar and liquid, this icing provides a glossy finish perfect for adding shimmering effects to your golem.

4. **Fondant and Edible Clay:**

    For more sculptural decorations, fondant or edible clay allows you to mold three-dimensional details, such as facial features or armor for your golem.

Recipe 1: Royal Icing for Precision and Strength
Ingredients:

- 3 cups powdered sugar, sifted
- 2 large egg whites (or 3 tablespoons meringue powder + 6 tablespoons water)
- 1 teaspoon lemon juice or vanilla extract

Instructions:

1. **Combine Ingredients:** In a clean, grease-free bowl, beat egg whites until frothy. Gradually add powdered sugar and lemon juice.
2. **Beat Until Stiff:** Mix on medium-high speed until the icing holds stiff peaks (about 5 minutes).
3. **Adjust Consistency:** Add a few drops of water for a thinner icing or more powdered sugar for a thicker paste, depending on your needs.

Pro Tips:

- Keep royal icing covered with a damp cloth to prevent it from hardening while you work.
- Use piping bags with small tips for detailed designs.

Recipe 2: Whipped Buttercream Frosting for Texture and Flavor

Ingredients:

- 1 cup unsalted butter, softened
- 4 cups powdered sugar, sifted
- 2 teaspoons vanilla extract
- 2–3 tablespoons heavy cream or milk

Instructions:

1. **Cream Butter:** Beat butter on medium speed until light and fluffy.
2. **Incorporate Sugar:** Gradually add powdered sugar, mixing well between additions.
3. **Add Liquid:** Stir in vanilla and cream, beating until smooth and spreadable.

Uses:

Buttercream is ideal for adding swirls, borders, or decorative textures, such as fur, feathers, or foliage.

Adding Enchantment: Coloring and Flavoring Frosting

To imbue your frostings with magical appeal, color and flavor are essential:

1. **Natural Food Coloring:**
   Use beet juice for reds, turmeric for yellows, matcha powder for greens, and butterfly pea powder for blues. These not only provide vivid colors but also tie into the magical, natural theme of your creation.
2. **Flavored Extracts and Oils:**
   Add a drop of peppermint, orange, almond, or rose extract to

give your frosting a unique twist. For an extra magical touch, consider floral flavors like lavender or hibiscus.

3. **Shimmer and Sparkle:**
Edible luster dust, glitter, and metallic powders can be mixed with frostings to create dazzling, otherworldly effects.

Edible Paints: Techniques for Detailed Magic

Edible paints allow you to bring depth, texture, and vibrancy to your Gingerbread Golem. They are particularly useful for creating lifelike details such as eyes, armor, or runes. Here's how to make and use edible paints:

Recipe: Basic Edible Paint
Ingredients:

- 2 tablespoons vodka or clear extract (e.g., lemon or almond extract)
- Edible food coloring gel
- Edible metallic powders (optional)

Instructions:

1. **Mix Paint:** In a small dish, combine a few drops of food coloring with the vodka or extract. For metallic effects, add a pinch of edible powder.
2. **Adjust Consistency:** Add more liquid for a watercolor effect or more gel/powder for a thicker paint.
3. **Apply with Brushes:** Use fine-tipped food-safe brushes to paint intricate designs.

Techniques for Decorating with Frosting and Paints

1. **Layering for Depth:**
   Begin with a base layer of frosting or paint to define large sections of your golem. Once dry, add smaller details like facial expressions, clothing, or runes.
2. **Stenciling Runes and Patterns:**
   Use stencils to create magical runes or repeating patterns. Hold the stencil firmly over the gingerbread piece and gently apply frosting or paint with a spatula or brush.
3. **Piping for Precision:**
   Use royal icing in piping bags with fine tips to outline features, add borders, or draw intricate designs.
4. **Blending Colors:**
   For a mystical, gradient effect, blend edible paints on a damp surface. This technique works well for creating ombre patterns or the appearance of glowing energy.

Magical Design Ideas for Your Gingerbread Golem

- **Runic Armor:** Paint protective symbols or magical runes onto the body of your golem using metallic edible paint.
- **Shimmering Eyes:** Use edible glitter and a dot of royal icing to create lifelike, sparkling eyes that bring your golem to life.
- **Frosted Energy Lines:** Pipe glowing "energy" patterns in neon-colored royal icing to make your golem look otherworldly.
- **Sugary Accessories:** Sculpt accessories like hats, staffs, or shields using fondant or edible clay, then paint them with metallic accents.

Troubleshooting Frosting and Paint Challenges

- **Icing Too Runny:** Add powdered sugar to thicken it. For royal icing, ensure you're beating it long enough for stiff peaks.
- **Paint Not Sticking:** Make sure the surface of your gingerbread is clean and smooth. For better adherence, use a thin layer of royal icing as a primer.
- **Colors Bleeding:** Allow each layer of frosting or paint to dry fully before adding another.

Frostings and edible paints are more than just decorative elements; they are the artistic tools that transform a simple gingerbread creation into a magical masterpiece. With these recipes, techniques, and ideas, you'll be able to give your Gingerbread Golem a dazzling, enchanted finish that captivates both the eye and the imagination. Let your creativity guide you as you breathe life—and a little magic—into your creation.

Chapter 3: Spiced Golem Hearts – Magical Fillings and Centers

At the core of every Gingerbread Golem lies its "heart"—a magical center that transforms your creation into a masterpiece of flavor and mystery. The heart of your golem isn't just a delicious filling; it represents its essence, the hidden magic that brings your edible guardian to life. This chapter explores the art of creating enchanting centers, from molten chocolate to spiced caramel and enchanted fruit preserves, designed to delight your senses and elevate your golem to mythical status.

The Symbolism of a Golem's Heart

In folklore, the heart of a golem represents its energy source, the element that imbues it with life and purpose. In your Gingerbread Golem, the heart is a literal and metaphorical focal point, where bold flavors and magical textures reside. Crafting the perfect center involves balancing taste, texture, and visual allure, ensuring each bite is an unforgettable experience.

Choosing the Right Filling for Your Golem

Different fillings evoke different moods and magical properties. Consider these options:

1. **Spiced Caramel:**
   Representing warmth and strength, spiced caramel brings a rich, velvety texture and a blend of spices that enhance the gingerbread's flavor.

2. **Molten Chocolate:**
   A luxurious and decadent choice, molten chocolate symbolizes the hidden depths of your golem's magic. Dark chocolate adds an air of mystery, while milk chocolate offers a sweeter touch.

3. **Enchanted Fruit Preserves:**
   Bright, tangy fruit preserves bring a burst of life and color to your golem, evoking the vitality of the natural world. Enhanced with edible glitter or a touch of spice, they can mimic the shimmer of a magical core.

4. **Nut and Spiced Honey Paste:**
A filling made from ground nuts and spiced honey symbolizes abundance and resilience, perfect for golems meant to invoke protection or prosperity.

Recipe 1: Spiced Caramel Filling
Ingredients:

- 1 cup granulated sugar
- 6 tablespoons unsalted butter, cubed
- ½ cup heavy cream
- 1 teaspoon ground cinnamon
- ¼ teaspoon ground nutmeg
- 1 pinch of ground cloves
- 1 teaspoon vanilla extract

Instructions:

1. **Melt the Sugar:** In a medium saucepan, heat sugar over medium heat, stirring constantly until it melts into a golden-brown liquid.
2. **Add Butter:** Carefully add butter, whisking continuously. The mixture will bubble vigorously—this is normal.
3. **Incorporate Cream:** Slowly pour in the heavy cream, continuing to whisk. Reduce heat to low and cook for 2–3 minutes until the mixture thickens.
4. **Add Spices and Vanilla:** Stir in cinnamon, nutmeg, cloves, and vanilla. Allow the caramel to cool slightly before using it as a filling.

Tips:

- For extra magic, stir in edible glitter once the caramel cools.

- Use a piping bag to neatly fill your gingerbread pieces with the caramel.

Recipe 2: Molten Chocolate Filling
Ingredients:

- 4 ounces dark chocolate (70% cocoa or higher), chopped
- ½ cup heavy cream
- 1 tablespoon unsalted butter
- 1 teaspoon ground cinnamon
- 1 pinch of chili powder (optional, for a magical "kick")

Instructions:

1. **Heat the Cream:** In a small saucepan, warm the cream over medium heat until it just begins to simmer.
2. **Add Chocolate and Butter:** Remove from heat and add the chopped chocolate and butter. Let sit for 1 minute, then whisk until smooth.
3. **Incorporate Spices:** Stir in cinnamon and chili powder (if using). Allow the mixture to cool slightly before filling.

Tips:

- For a molten effect, bake filled pieces briefly to allow the chocolate to melt slightly before serving.
- Pair this filling with a dark chocolate drizzle for extra indulgence.

Recipe 3: Enchanted Fruit Preserves
Ingredients:

- 1 cup fruit of choice (berries, stone fruits, or citrus work well)
- ½ cup granulated sugar
- 1 tablespoon lemon juice
- 1 teaspoon ground ginger
- ½ teaspoon ground cardamom
- 1 teaspoon edible glitter (optional)

Instructions:

1. **Cook the Fruit:** In a saucepan, combine the fruit, sugar, and lemon juice. Cook over medium heat until the fruit softens and begins to release its juices.
2. **Add Spices:** Stir in ginger and cardamom, then reduce the heat and simmer until the mixture thickens to a jam-like consistency.
3. **Cool and Add Glitter:** Let the preserves cool, then stir in edible glitter for a magical sparkle.

Tips:

- Use vibrant fruits like raspberries, blackberries, or apricots to create visually striking centers.
- Strain the mixture for a smoother filling if desired.

Filling Techniques for Your Golem

The method of filling your Gingerbread Golem depends on its design and purpose. Here are some approaches:

1. **Hollow Centers:**
   For larger golem pieces, carve out a hollow space before baking and fill it with your chosen mixture. Seal the opening with royal icing after filling.
2. **Layering:**
   Use a thin layer of filling sandwiched between two pieces of gingerbread to create a stable and visually appealing design.
3. **Piping:**
   Use a piping bag fitted with a small tip to inject fillings into the center of gingerbread figures or decorative elements.
4. **Hidden Cores:**
   For a surprise effect, bake a small sphere of filling (e.g., frozen caramel or chocolate ganache) into the center of a thick gingerbread piece.

Enhancing the Magical Appeal

To amplify the enchantment of your Gingerbread Golem's heart, consider these ideas:

- **Shimmering Effects:** Add edible glitter or metallic dust to your filling for a magical, glowing effect when the golem is broken apart.
- **Flavor Infusions:** Infuse your fillings with herbs like lavender, rosemary, or mint for an unexpected and mystical flavor profile.
- **Color Contrasts:** Use brightly colored fillings to create a striking contrast with the gingerbread exterior.

Troubleshooting Common Issues

- **Runny Fillings:** Thicken runny fillings with cornstarch or cook them longer to evaporate excess liquid.
- **Leakage:** Ensure your gingerbread pieces are fully sealed around the filling using royal icing or additional dough.
- **Hard Fillings:** For softer textures, avoid overcooking caramel or chocolate.

Conclusion

The heart of your Gingerbread Golem is more than a filling—it's a symbol of its magical essence. By carefully selecting and crafting your golem's center, you can create a unique and flavorful experience that enhances the story and charm of your creation. Whether it's the rich allure of molten chocolate, the comforting warmth of spiced caramel, or the vibrant burst of enchanted fruit preserves, these magical fillings will captivate and delight all who encounter your golem.

Chapter 4: Alchemical Bakes – Infusing Spices and Herbs

In the mystical art of gingerbread alchemy, the proper selection and infusion of spices and herbs is key to creating a flavor profile that is both enchanting and deeply satisfying. Spices and herbs are more than just ingredients—they carry ancient histories, symbolic meanings, and even perceived magical properties. In this chapter, we'll delve into the secrets of combining these aromatic treasures to infuse your Gingerbread Golem with unique flavors and a touch of magical energy.

The Magical Properties of Spices and Herbs

In many cultures, spices and herbs are believed to carry mystical energies that align with various intentions, from protection and abundance to passion and clarity. Here's a brief overview of some key spices and herbs to use in your alchemical bakes:

1. Cardamom – The Sweet Awakener

- **Flavor Profile:** Warm, citrusy, and slightly floral.
- **Magical Properties:** Associated with awakening creativity, enhancing intuition, and fostering love.
- **Culinary Use:** Balances sweetness with a subtle brightness; excellent in gingerbread for a nuanced depth.

2. Anise – The Star of Protection

- **Flavor Profile:** Sweet, licorice-like, and slightly peppery.
- **Magical Properties:** Linked to warding off negativity, protection, and boosting psychic abilities.

- **Culinary Use:** Ideal for adding a distinct aromatic twist; pairs well with cloves and cinnamon.

3. Nutmeg – The Spice of Abundance

- **Flavor Profile:** Earthy, warm, and slightly nutty with sweet undertones.
- **Magical Properties:** Tied to prosperity, luck, and grounding energy.
- **Culinary Use:** A classic in gingerbread, it enhances warmth and balances other spices.

4. Cinnamon – The Flame of Vitality

- **Flavor Profile:** Sweet, woody, and slightly spicy.
- **Magical Properties:** Represents passion, protection, and spiritual strength.
- **Culinary Use:** A cornerstone of gingerbread, cinnamon harmonizes with almost any spice.

5. Clove – The Guardian Spice

- **Flavor Profile:** Intensely aromatic, warm, and slightly bitter.
- **Magical Properties:** Used for protection, healing, and invoking courage.
- **Culinary Use:** Adds a deep, spicy heat and complements sweet and savory flavors.

6. Ginger – The Root of Fire

- **Flavor Profile:** Sharp, zesty, and slightly sweet.
- **Magical Properties:** Encourages vitality, prosperity, and bold action.

- **Culinary Use:** The heart of gingerbread; its fiery warmth is unmistakable.

7. Herbs – The Subtle Enhancers

- **Lavender:** Adds a floral note and promotes peace and calm.
- **Rosemary:** Sharp, pine-like aroma; symbolizes clarity and protection.
- **Mint:** Cooling and refreshing; associated with renewal and abundance.

Creating the Perfect Spice Blend

A well-balanced spice blend is the soul of a Gingerbread Golem. The proportions of each spice can be adjusted to suit your preferences or the magical intention you wish to infuse. Here's a base recipe to get you started:

Magical Gingerbread Spice Blend

- 3 tablespoons ground cinnamon
- 1 tablespoon ground ginger
- 1 teaspoon ground nutmeg
- ½ teaspoon ground cloves
- ½ teaspoon ground cardamom
- ½ teaspoon ground anise

Instructions:

1. Combine all spices in a bowl, whisking thoroughly to ensure even distribution.
2. Store in an airtight container for up to 6 months.
3. Use 2–3 teaspoons of the blend per batch of gingerbread dough, or adjust to taste.

Infusing Herbs into Your Gingerbread

Herbs can add subtle depth and complexity to your gingerbread, either as part of the dough or incorporated into fillings and toppings.

Infusion Techniques

1. **Herbal Syrups:**
   Create a simple syrup infused with herbs like lavender or rosemary. Add it to your dough or glaze for a subtle flavor.

Recipe:

-
    - 1 cup water
    - 1 cup sugar
    - 2 tablespoons dried herbs (e.g., lavender or rosemary)
    - Simmer water and sugar until dissolved, then steep herbs for 15 minutes. Strain and use.

1. **Herbal Extracts:**
   Mint, lemon balm, or thyme extracts can be made at home by steeping fresh herbs in vodka for a few weeks. Add a few drops to your gingerbread mix.
2. **Herb-Infused Butter or Oil:**
   Melt butter or warm neutral oil and steep fresh herbs for an hour. Strain and use in your recipe for subtle, earthy notes.

Recipes for Alchemical Infusions
Recipe 1: Rosemary-Lavender Gingerbread Dough
Ingredients:

- 2 tablespoons dried lavender
- 1 tablespoon finely chopped fresh rosemary
- 3 teaspoons Magical Gingerbread Spice Blend (see above)

Instructions:

1. Grind lavender and rosemary into a fine powder using a spice grinder or mortar and pestle.
2. Mix into the dry ingredients of your gingerbread dough recipe.
3. Proceed with the recipe as usual, enjoying the floral and pine-like aromas during baking.

Recipe 2: Spiced Honey Glaze with Mint
Ingredients:

- ½ cup honey
- 1 tablespoon chopped fresh mint leaves
- ½ teaspoon cinnamon
- 1 pinch of nutmeg

Instructions:

1. Warm honey in a small saucepan over low heat.
2. Stir in mint leaves and spices. Simmer for 5 minutes.
3. Strain to remove mint leaves and drizzle over baked gingerbread pieces.

Recipe 3: Anise-Cardamom Royal Icing
Ingredients:

- 2 cups powdered sugar
- 1 egg white or 2 tablespoons meringue powder + 2 tablespoons water
- ¼ teaspoon ground anise
- ¼ teaspoon ground cardamom

Instructions:

1. Beat egg white until frothy, then gradually add powdered sugar.
2. Stir in spices and mix until smooth.
3. Use for piping intricate designs or as a magical adhesive for your Golem.

Balancing Flavors and Aromas

Combining spices and herbs requires a delicate touch to avoid overpowering flavors. Here are some tips:

- **Start Small:** Begin with small amounts of strong spices like cloves or anise and adjust gradually.
- **Balance Sweet and Savory:** Herbs like rosemary or thyme pair well with sweet gingerbread, adding a surprising depth.
- **Layer Flavors:** Use different spices in the dough, filling, and glaze for a multi-dimensional flavor experience.

Troubleshooting Spice and Herb Infusions

- **Overpowering Flavors:** If a spice dominates, balance it with a neutral flavor like vanilla or a touch of citrus.
- **Bitter Notes:** Over-brewed herbs can taste bitter; steep for shorter periods or use smaller quantities.

- **Uneven Distribution:** Always mix spice blends thoroughly to avoid concentrated patches in your dough.

Enhancing the Magic

Infusing your Gingerbread Golem with spices and herbs isn't just about flavor—it's about imbuing your creation with intention and energy. As you mix and bake, focus on the magical properties of each ingredient, visualizing the energy you want to impart. Whether it's protection, joy, or creativity, your Gingerbread Golem will carry the essence of your intention in every bite.

By mastering the alchemical art of spice and herb infusion, you're not just baking—you're crafting an edible masterpiece that honors tradition, awakens the senses, and inspires wonder.

Chapter 5: Golem Guardians – Miniature Companion Treats

In the enchanting world of the Gingerbread Golem, the larger-than-life protector doesn't stand alone. Miniature companion golems, crafted from the same magical dough and infused with similar intent, serve as loyal guardians, playful decorations, or thoughtful edible gifts. These small golems not only enhance your holiday table's charm but also carry the same warmth and protective symbolism as their larger counterpart.

This chapter focuses on creating miniature golems, including their design, assembly, and decoration. Whether they're whimsical table guardians, edible placeholders, or intricate ornaments, these small figures will add a magical touch to your celebrations.

The Role of Miniature Golem Guardians

In folklore, smaller golems often accompanied larger ones, acting as assistants or sentinels. In your edible world, these tiny creations can serve various purposes:

1. **Table Guardians:** Position them around your centerpiece to "guard" your feast.
2. **Placeholders:** Personalize them with names to serve as charming edible placeholders for guests.
3. **Ornaments:** Add ribbons or stands to turn them into delightful holiday decorations.
4. **Gifts:** Package them in decorative boxes as unique and thoughtful presents.

Planning Your Miniature Golem Design

Before diving into the baking process, decide on the role and design of your miniature golems. Here are some ideas to inspire you:

1. **Traditional Guardians:** Classic gingerbread shapes—like humanoid figures with small shields, staffs, or swords.
2. **Whimsical Creatures:** Miniature animals, mythical creatures, or even hybrid designs (e.g., part animal, part human).
3. **Holiday-Themed:** Santa hats, reindeer antlers, or snowflake accessories to tie them to the festive season.

Perfect Dough for Miniature Golems

Miniature golems require a sturdy yet pliable dough that can hold intricate details. Use the same base recipe from *Chapter 1: Building the Foundation* but adjust the thickness:

- Roll the dough to about **⅛ inch** thick for delicate designs.
- For sturdier figures, use **¼ inch** thickness.

Crafting Miniature Golems: Step-by-Step Process
Step 1: Shaping and Cutting

1. **Templates:** Create paper templates for custom designs, or use cookie cutters for basic shapes.
2. **Freehand Details:** Use small, sharp knives or specialized fondant tools to carve features like arms, legs, or facial details directly into the dough.

Step 2: Baking

1. **Chill Before Baking:** After shaping, chill the dough for 15–20 minutes to help retain fine details.
2. **Bake on Parchment:** Bake at 350°F (175°C) for 8–10 minutes, depending on the size and thickness. Watch closely to avoid over-browning.

Decorating Miniature Golems
Once baked and cooled, decorating these tiny guardians is where creativity truly shines.
Royal Icing for Fine Details
Royal icing is perfect for adding facial expressions, clothing, and accessories. Use fine-tipped piping bags for precision.
Pro Tips:

- Use contrasting colors for definition. For example, white icing outlines and red accessories create festive designs.
- Layer icing for a 3D effect, allowing each layer to dry before adding the next.

Edible Paints for Customization

Use edible paints to add shimmer, metallic effects, or intricate patterns like runes and symbols.

Accessories and Embellishments

1. **Candy Shields and Weapons:**
    - Use peppermint sticks for staffs or candy canes for miniature weapons.
    - Cut small discs from fondant to create shields and decorate with edible glitter or paint.
2. **Ribbons and Tags:**

    For placeholders or gifts, tie a ribbon around the neck or waist of each golem and attach a small name tag.
3. **Eyes and Faces:**
    - Use tiny dots of melted chocolate or royal icing for eyes.
    - Add character with curved icing for smiles or frowns, depending on the personality you want to convey.

Turning Miniature Golems into Decorations

Transform your edible creations into lasting keepsakes:

1. **Ornaments:**
     - Poke a small hole at the top of each golem before baking.
     - Once cooled, thread a ribbon through the hole for hanging.
2. **Table Centerpieces:**
     - Arrange a group of miniature golems around a larger Gingerbread Golem as a "golem army."
     - Add battery-powered tea lights to create a glowing, magical effect.
3. **Gifts:**
     - Package miniature golems in cellophane bags with a festive ribbon.
     - Include a small card explaining their magical role as table guardians.

Specialty Miniature Golem Recipes
Recipe 1: Chocolate-Peppermint Mini Golems
Ingredients:

- 1 cup all-purpose flour
- ½ cup cocoa powder
- 1 teaspoon baking soda
- 1 teaspoon ground cinnamon
- ¼ teaspoon ground cloves
- ½ cup unsalted butter
- ½ cup granulated sugar
- 1 egg
- 1 teaspoon peppermint extract

Instructions:

1. Prepare dough as described in Chapter 1, incorporating cocoa powder and peppermint extract.
2. Shape and bake as outlined above.
3. Decorate with red and white royal icing to create a candy cane-inspired design.

Recipe 2: Spiced Almond Mini Golems
Ingredients:

- 2 cups almond flour
- 1 cup all-purpose flour
- 1 teaspoon ground cardamom
- 1 teaspoon ground cinnamon
- ½ cup honey
- ½ cup unsalted butter

Instructions:

1. Combine dry ingredients in a bowl.
2. Heat honey and butter until melted; mix into dry ingredients to form a dough.
3. Shape, bake, and decorate with gold luster dust for an enchanted, regal look.

Troubleshooting Miniature Golems

- **Cracked Dough:** Ensure your dough is properly chilled and not overworked.
- **Collapsed Shapes:** Use thicker dough or reinforce delicate parts with additional dough or icing.
- **Uneven Baking:** Rotate baking sheets halfway through for even browning.

Enhancing the Magic of Miniature Golems

To infuse your miniature golems with symbolic meaning, focus on their role in your celebration:

- **Guardians:** Add protective runes or symbols using edible paint.
- **Messengers:** Write personalized messages on ribbons or tags.
- **Companions:** Create animal-themed golems to accompany your main Gingerbread Golem.

By mastering the art of crafting miniature golems, you'll bring a layer of whimsy and wonder to your holiday traditions. These tiny protectors not only delight the eye but also carry the spirit of the season, reminding everyone at your table of the joy and creativity that comes with the art of baking.

Chapter 6: Sweet Rituals – Symbolic Cookies and Offerings

Throughout history, baked goods have carried symbolic significance, serving as offerings, charms, and talismans in rituals of protection, abundance, and celebration. These sweet creations transcend mere sustenance, acting as conduits of intention and energy. In this chapter, we'll explore how to craft ritualistic cookies infused with meaning, using symbolic shapes and purposeful recipes to honor traditions, manifest desires, and elevate your Gingerbread Golem experience.

The Power of Symbolic Baking

Symbolic baking is an ancient practice found in many cultures. From the braided challah of Jewish tradition to the sun-shaped bread of pagan Yule celebrations, these edible creations often represent deeper meanings. When crafting ritual cookies, the shape, ingredients, and method of preparation are imbued with intention, turning each cookie into a vessel of magic.

Symbolic Shapes and Their Meanings

Choosing the right shape for your ritual cookies is essential to aligning them with your purpose:

1. **Circles:** Represent unity, eternity, and protection. Perfect for invoking harmony or creating boundaries of safety.
2. **Stars:** Symbolize guidance, hope, and celestial power. Ideal for celebrating personal achievements or the return of light during the winter solstice.
3. **Hearts:** Represent love, connection, and emotional healing. Use for rituals involving relationships or self-love.
4. **Animals:** Different animals carry specific energies—owls for wisdom, bears for strength, and deer for gentleness.
5. **Runes and Sigils:** Etch magical symbols into your cookies to amplify their intent, whether it's for protection, abundance, or clarity.
6. **Wreaths:** A circle adorned with patterns, symbolizing cycles and renewal, perfect for celebrations of new beginnings.

Ritualistic Cookie Doughs and Their Properties

The dough used for your symbolic cookies can enhance their meaning. Below are some traditional and magical dough bases:

Gingerbread Dough:

Symbolizes warmth, strength, and protection. Its spiced aroma invokes a sense of comfort and grounding.

Honey-Almond Dough:

Represents sweetness and prosperity. Almonds are often associated with abundance and wisdom, while honey embodies the richness of life.

Oatmeal Dough:

Associated with grounding and stability. Oats have long been a symbol of nourishment and security.

Recipe 1: Sunburst Cookies for Abundance
Ingredients:

- 2 cups all-purpose flour
- 1 teaspoon ground turmeric (for golden color and abundance energy)
- 1 teaspoon ground cinnamon
- ½ teaspoon ground ginger
- ½ cup unsalted butter, softened
- ½ cup honey
- 1 large egg

Instructions:

1. **Prepare the Dough:** Cream the butter and honey together. Add the egg and mix well. Gradually incorporate the dry ingredients, forming a soft dough.
2. **Shape the Sunbursts:** Roll out the dough to ¼-inch thickness. Use a star-shaped cutter, or create a circle and score radiating lines to resemble a sun.
3. **Bake:** Preheat the oven to 350°F (175°C) and bake for 10–12 minutes, or until the edges are golden.
4. **Decorate:** Dust with edible gold dust or drizzle with honey glaze to enhance the radiant effect.

Recipe 2: Rune-Engraved Protection Cookies
Ingredients:

- 1 ½ cups all-purpose flour
- ½ cup almond flour
- 1 teaspoon ground cloves (for protective energy)
- ½ teaspoon ground nutmeg
- ½ cup unsalted butter
- ½ cup granulated sugar
- 1 teaspoon vanilla extract

Instructions:

1. **Prepare the Dough:** Mix the dry ingredients in one bowl. Cream the butter and sugar, then add the vanilla. Combine wet and dry ingredients to form a firm dough.
2. **Shape the Cookies:** Roll out the dough to ¼-inch thickness. Use a round cutter or freehand shapes.
3. **Engrave the Runes:** Before baking, use a skewer or the edge of a small knife to carve protective runes or sigils into the dough.
4. **Bake:** Bake at 350°F (175°C) for 8–10 minutes, watching carefully to preserve the runes' details.

Recipe 3: Spiral Wreath Cookies for Celebration
Ingredients:

- 2 cups all-purpose flour
- ½ cup powdered sugar
- 1 cup unsalted butter, softened
- 1 teaspoon almond extract
- 2 tablespoons cocoa powder (optional, for a dual-color spiral effect)

Instructions:

1. **Divide the Dough:** Cream the butter and sugar, then mix in the flour and almond extract. Split the dough into two halves, adding cocoa powder to one for a contrasting color.
2. **Create Spirals:** Roll each half into a thin rectangle. Place one on top of the other and roll tightly into a spiral. Chill for 30 minutes.
3. **Slice and Shape:** Slice the roll into ¼-inch thick rounds. Shape the rounds into mini wreaths by forming a circle.
4. **Bake:** Preheat the oven to 350°F (175°C) and bake for 10–12 minutes.
5. **Decorate:** Add edible glitter or small sugar pearls to mimic festive decorations.

Ritual Preparation and Baking Tips

- **Set Your Intention:** Before beginning, take a moment to focus on your goal for the cookies, whether it's protection, abundance, or celebration.
- **Bless the Ingredients:** Infuse your spices and dough with your intent by holding your hands over them and visualizing your desired outcome.
- **Bake in Silence or with Music:** Create a sacred atmosphere while baking, playing music that aligns with your intention or working in peaceful silence.

Using Symbolic Cookies in Rituals

1. **As Offerings:** Place the cookies on an altar or outdoor space as offerings to spirits, deities, or the earth.
2. **For Sharing:** Share the cookies with loved ones, symbolizing the spread of protection or joy.
3. **For Meditation:** Eat a cookie mindfully during meditation, focusing on the flavor and the intention behind it.
4. **In Decor:** Arrange the cookies on your table or tree to invoke the desired energy throughout your home.

Troubleshooting Symbolic Cookie Challenges

- **Fading Shapes:** Chill your dough before baking and avoid over-baking to preserve intricate details.
- **Uneven Color:** Rotate your baking tray halfway through for even browning.
- **Broken Edges:** Use a slightly thicker dough for delicate shapes to prevent breakage.

The Magic of Sweet Rituals

Symbolic cookies are more than treats; they are expressions of creativity and intention. By shaping dough into meaningful forms and infusing it with purposeful ingredients, you can create magical offerings that nourish the body and spirit alike. These recipes and techniques invite you to celebrate the season with rituals that honor tradition, foster connection, and bring a little extra magic to your table.

So roll out your dough, let your imagination take flight, and craft cookies that are as powerful as they are delicious. Your Gingerbread Golem will thank you for the company of these sweet, symbolic guardians!

Chapter 7: Holiday Spells in a Mug – Gingerbread Drinks and Elixirs

There's something magical about a warm drink on a frosty winter day. When infused with the rich, spiced flavors of gingerbread, these beverages become more than just comforting treats—they transform into elixirs that soothe the soul, spark joy, and invite the spirit of the season into every sip. In this chapter, we'll explore a variety of gingerbread-inspired drinks, from decadent spiced cocoa to aromatic mulled cider and enchanting lattes, each crafted with intention and care.

The Magic of Gingerbread Flavors in Beverages

Gingerbread's distinctive blend of spices—ginger, cinnamon, nutmeg, and cloves—awakens the senses and evokes the warmth of the holidays. When these flavors are paired with beverages, they create an immersive experience that is both aromatic and flavorful. Beyond their taste, the spices carry symbolic meanings, turning each drink into a spell in a mug:

- **Ginger:** Energy, vitality, and prosperity.
- **Cinnamon:** Passion, protection, and abundance.
- **Nutmeg:** Luck, clarity, and warmth.
- **Cloves:** Healing, courage, and spiritual strength.

By combining these flavors with warm bases like milk, coffee, tea, or cider, you can create drinks that comfort and inspire.

Crafting the Perfect Gingerbread Spice Blend

Before diving into the recipes, prepare a gingerbread spice mix to have on hand for quick and consistent flavoring.

Gingerbread Spice Blend:

- 3 tablespoons ground cinnamon
- 2 tablespoons ground ginger
- 1 teaspoon ground nutmeg
- ½ teaspoon ground cloves
- ½ teaspoon ground cardamom (optional, for an extra aromatic kick)

Mix all ingredients thoroughly and store in an airtight container. Use this blend to flavor drinks, desserts, or even savory dishes.

Recipe 1: Gingerbread Spiced Cocoa
Ingredients:

- 2 cups whole milk (or plant-based alternative)
- 3 tablespoons unsweetened cocoa powder
- 2 tablespoons granulated sugar (or sweetener of choice)
- 1 teaspoon gingerbread spice blend
- 1 teaspoon vanilla extract
- Whipped cream (optional)
- Crushed gingerbread cookies (for garnish)

Instructions:

1. **Heat the Milk:** In a medium saucepan, warm the milk over medium heat until it begins to steam (but do not boil).
2. **Mix the Cocoa:** Whisk together the cocoa powder, sugar, and gingerbread spice blend in a small bowl. Gradually add to the milk, whisking constantly to dissolve.
3. **Add Vanilla:** Stir in the vanilla extract and remove from heat.
4. **Serve:** Pour into mugs, top with whipped cream, and sprinkle with crushed gingerbread cookies for a festive touch.

Recipe 2: Gingerbread Latte
Ingredients:

- 1 cup strong brewed coffee or 1 shot of espresso
- 1 cup milk (or plant-based alternative)
- 2 tablespoons gingerbread syrup (recipe included below)
- Whipped cream (optional)
- Ground cinnamon or nutmeg (for garnish)

Instructions:

1. **Prepare the Gingerbread Syrup:** Combine ½ cup water, ½ cup sugar, 1 tablespoon gingerbread spice blend, and 1 teaspoon molasses in a small saucepan. Simmer over low heat until the sugar dissolves and the mixture thickens slightly (about 5 minutes). Strain and cool.
2. **Steam the Milk:** Heat the milk until frothy using a steamer or stovetop.
3. **Assemble the Latte:** Pour the gingerbread syrup into a mug, add the coffee or espresso, and top with steamed milk.
4. **Garnish:** Add whipped cream and sprinkle with cinnamon or nutmeg for a festive flair.

Recipe 3: Mulled Gingerbread Cider
Ingredients:

- 4 cups apple cider
- 1 orange, sliced
- 2 cinnamon sticks
- 1 teaspoon gingerbread spice blend
- 5–6 whole cloves
- 2 tablespoons honey or brown sugar (optional)
- Star anise (for garnish)

Instructions:

1. **Simmer the Cider:** In a large pot, combine the cider, orange slices, cinnamon sticks, gingerbread spice blend, cloves, and honey or sugar (if using).
2. **Heat Slowly:** Warm the mixture over low heat for 20–30 minutes, allowing the spices to infuse.
3. **Strain and Serve:** Remove the orange slices and cloves. Pour into mugs and garnish with a star anise for a dramatic, aromatic presentation.

Recipe 4: Gingerbread Chai Latte
Ingredients:

- 2 cups water
- 2 black tea bags (or loose-leaf tea equivalent)
- 1 cup milk (or plant-based alternative)
- 1 tablespoon gingerbread spice blend
- 1 tablespoon brown sugar or honey
- ½ teaspoon vanilla extract

Instructions:

1. **Brew the Tea:** Bring the water to a boil in a small saucepan. Add the tea bags and gingerbread spice blend, then reduce the heat and simmer for 5 minutes.
2. **Add Milk and Sweetener:** Stir in the milk and brown sugar or honey. Simmer for an additional 2–3 minutes.
3. **Strain and Serve:** Remove the tea bags and pour the mixture through a strainer to remove spices. Add vanilla extract and serve hot.

Recipe 5: Frosty Gingerbread Milkshake (Optional Cold Option)

Ingredients:

- 2 cups vanilla ice cream
- 1 cup milk (or plant-based alternative)
- 1 tablespoon gingerbread spice blend
- 1 teaspoon molasses
- Whipped cream (optional)
- Crushed gingerbread cookies (for garnish)

Instructions:

1. **Blend the Ingredients:** Combine the ice cream, milk, gingerbread spice blend, and molasses in a blender. Blend until smooth.
2. **Serve:** Pour into a glass, top with whipped cream, and garnish with crushed gingerbread cookies for a festive look.

Enhancing the Magic of Gingerbread Drinks

These drinks are more than delightful beverages—they can also carry symbolic or ritualistic meanings. Here's how to amplify their magic:

1. **Set an Intention:** As you prepare your drink, focus on the purpose you want to imbue into it—be it warmth, joy, or connection.
2. **Use a Special Mug:** Serve your drink in a favorite or meaningful mug to enhance its personal significance.
3. **Stir Clockwise:** Stirring clockwise is thought to bring in positive energy, while stirring counterclockwise is used to release negativity.
4. **Share the Magic:** Offer these drinks to friends and family, spreading the warmth and intention you've infused.

Troubleshooting Common Issues

- **Lumps in Cocoa:** Whisk the dry ingredients thoroughly before adding to the milk, and whisk constantly while heating.
- **Overly Sweet Drinks:** Adjust sugar levels to taste or use unsweetened alternatives like dark chocolate or black tea.
- **Weak Spices:** Simmer longer or add a pinch more gingerbread spice blend to intensify the flavor.

Conclusion

Holiday beverages infused with gingerbread flavors are the perfect way to warm your heart and soul. Whether you're sipping spiced cocoa by the fire, enjoying a gingerbread latte with friends, or filling your home with the scent of mulled cider, these drinks invite the magic of the season into every moment. With their rich flavors and symbolic spices, these elixirs will become cherished rituals in your holiday celebrations.

Chapter 8: Beyond the Oven – No-Bake Golem Creations

For those who want to enjoy the magic of gingerbread flavors without turning on the oven, no-bake recipes offer a versatile and creative solution. These alternatives capture the essence of gingerbread while providing unique textures and presentation styles. From decadent truffles to layered parfaits, these creations are perfect for busy schedules, non-bakers, or anyone looking to experiment with new ways to enjoy this classic holiday flavor.

The Appeal of No-Bake Golem Creations

No-bake recipes are not just easy to prepare; they also allow for creativity and flexibility in presentation. These desserts can be crafted into miniature golems, layered works of art, or simple treats infused with gingerbread-inspired flavors. Without the need for an oven, you can involve children, experiment with shapes, or prepare desserts on short notice while still honoring the rich traditions of gingerbread.

Key Ingredients for No-Bake Creations

The foundation of no-bake recipes lies in selecting the right ingredients to mimic the flavors and textures of baked gingerbread.

1. **Gingerbread Spices:** Cinnamon, ginger, nutmeg, cloves, and cardamom create the signature warmth.
2. **Crushed Cookies or Crackers:** Gingersnaps, graham crackers, or digestive biscuits provide the base for many no-bake desserts.
3. **Creamy Elements:** Cream cheese, whipped cream, or yogurt help bind and add richness.
4. **Sweeteners:** Honey, molasses, or brown sugar enhance the gingerbread flavor.
5. **Decorative Toppings:** Crushed cookies, edible glitter, or frosting add a festive touch.

Recipe 1: Gingerbread Truffles
Ingredients:

- 1 ½ cups crushed gingersnap cookies
- 4 ounces cream cheese, softened
- 1 tablespoon molasses
- 1 teaspoon gingerbread spice blend
- 8 ounces white or dark chocolate, melted (for coating)
- Edible glitter or sprinkles (optional)

Instructions:

1. **Prepare the Base:** In a bowl, combine crushed gingersnap cookies, cream cheese, molasses, and gingerbread spice blend. Mix until a dough-like consistency forms.
2. **Shape the Truffles:** Roll the mixture into small balls (about 1 inch in diameter) and place them on a parchment-lined baking sheet. Chill in the freezer for 15–20 minutes.
3. **Coat the Truffles:** Dip each ball into the melted chocolate, ensuring an even coating. Place back on the parchment paper.
4. **Decorate:** Before the chocolate sets, sprinkle with edible glitter or sprinkles. Chill until firm.

Variations:

- Add finely chopped nuts or dried fruit for texture.
- Use dark chocolate for a richer flavor or white chocolate for a sweeter contrast.

Recipe 2: Gingerbread Parfaits
Ingredients:

- 2 cups crushed graham crackers or gingersnaps
- 1 cup whipped cream or whipped topping
- 1 cup vanilla yogurt
- 1 tablespoon molasses
- 1 teaspoon gingerbread spice blend
- Crushed cookies or edible decorations for topping

Instructions:

1. **Prepare the Cream:** In a bowl, combine whipped cream, yogurt, molasses, and gingerbread spice blend. Mix until smooth.
2. **Layer the Parfait:** In a clear glass or jar, alternate layers of crushed cookies and the gingerbread cream mixture. Repeat until the glass is full.
3. **Top and Decorate:** Finish with a dollop of whipped cream and a sprinkle of crushed cookies or edible decorations. Chill before serving.

Tips:

- Use small jars or glasses for individual servings.
- Add a drizzle of caramel or chocolate sauce for extra indulgence.

**Recipe 3: No-Bake Gingerbread Cheesecake Bars
Ingredients:**

- 2 cups crushed gingersnaps or graham crackers
- ½ cup unsalted butter, melted
- 16 ounces cream cheese, softened
- 1 cup powdered sugar
- 1 teaspoon vanilla extract
- 2 tablespoons molasses
- 1 teaspoon gingerbread spice blend
- Whipped cream or cookie crumbles for garnish

Instructions:

1. **Make the Crust:** Combine crushed cookies and melted butter in a bowl. Press the mixture firmly into the bottom of an 8x8-inch pan. Chill for 10 minutes.
2. **Prepare the Filling:** In a mixing bowl, beat cream cheese, powdered sugar, vanilla extract, molasses, and gingerbread spice blend until smooth and creamy.
3. **Assemble the Bars:** Spread the cream cheese mixture evenly over the crust. Chill for at least 2 hours or until set.
4. **Serve:** Slice into bars and garnish with whipped cream or cookie crumbles.

Recipe 4: Gingerbread Energy Bites
Ingredients:

- 1 cup rolled oats
- ½ cup almond butter or peanut butter
- 2 tablespoons molasses
- 1 teaspoon gingerbread spice blend
- 2 tablespoons mini chocolate chips (optional)

Instructions:

1. **Mix the Ingredients:** Combine all ingredients in a bowl and stir until well mixed.
2. **Shape the Bites:** Roll the mixture into small balls (about 1 inch in diameter).
3. **Chill:** Place the bites on a parchment-lined tray and chill for at least 30 minutes before serving.

Tips:

- Store in an airtight container in the refrigerator for up to a week.
- Add a tablespoon of chia seeds or flaxseed for added nutrition.

Recipe 5: Gingerbread Icebox Cake
Ingredients:

- 2 cups whipped cream or whipped topping
- 1 cup cream cheese, softened
- 2 tablespoons molasses
- 1 teaspoon gingerbread spice blend
- 1 package gingersnap cookies

Instructions:

1. **Prepare the Filling:** Beat together whipped cream, cream cheese, molasses, and gingerbread spice blend until smooth.
2. **Assemble the Cake:** In a loaf pan or shallow dish, layer the cookies and cream mixture, starting with cookies. Repeat until all ingredients are used, ending with the cream mixture.
3. **Chill:** Cover and refrigerate overnight. The cookies will soften into a cake-like texture.
4. **Serve:** Slice and serve, garnishing with crushed cookies or a drizzle of molasses.

Decorating No-Bake Golem Creations

Although these desserts aren't baked, they can still be decorated to resemble miniature golems or festive shapes:

- **Truffle Faces:** Use melted chocolate or icing to draw eyes and mouths on truffles, transforming them into edible golems.
- **Parfait Layers:** Create faces or patterns using layers of contrasting colors in parfaits.
- **Cheesecake Bars:** Pipe decorative runes or symbols onto the top layer with royal icing or melted chocolate.

Using No-Bake Treats as Edible Golem Accents

No-bake creations can complement larger baked gingerbread golems as smaller, decorative elements:

- **Truffle "Hearts":** Place a truffle inside the hollow of a larger golem as its "heart."
- **Parfait Golem Bases:** Use parfaits as edible pedestals for displaying baked golems.
- **Cheesecake Offerings:** Serve cheesecake bars as symbolic offerings beside your golem centerpiece.

Troubleshooting No-Bake Recipes

- **Crumbly Mixtures:** Add more binding ingredients like cream cheese, molasses, or nut butter to improve consistency.
- **Runny Layers:** Chill mixtures before assembling to ensure they hold their shape.
- **Uneven Layers:** Use a piping bag or spoon to create clean, even layers in parfaits and icebox cakes.

Conclusion

No-bake gingerbread creations are perfect for those who want to experiment with the flavors and magic of the season without the time or effort required for baking. These recipes are versatile, fun, and ideal for involving friends and family in the kitchen. From truffles to parfaits, these treats capture the essence of gingerbread while allowing you to explore new textures and presentations, all while celebrating the magic of the holidays.

Chapter 9: Golem Feast Centerpieces – Showstopper Confections

A Gingerbread Golem centerpiece is more than an edible creation; it's the focal point of your holiday feast, a culinary masterpiece that delights the eye, tantalizes the palate, and sparks conversation. These larger-than-life edible sculptures are a testament to your creativity and baking prowess, designed to anchor festive tables with their imposing presence and intricate details.

In this chapter, we'll walk you through designing, assembling, and decorating showstopper gingerbread golems that are equal parts art and dessert. From architectural considerations to finishing touches, you'll learn how to create a breathtaking centerpiece that steals the show.

Planning Your Gingerbread Golem Centerpiece

The first step in crafting a gingerbread golem is conceptualizing its design. A strong plan ensures your creation is structurally sound, visually stunning, and manageable within your skill level.

Design Considerations

1. **Theme:** Decide on the aesthetic for your golem. Options include:
     - **Traditional Protector:** A humanoid golem with runic details and festive attire.
     - **Whimsical Golem:** Playful elements like candy cane limbs or a gumdrop crown.
     - **Mythical Creature:** A dragon, griffin, or other fantastical being in gingerbread form.
2. **Size:** Ensure your golem's size is proportional to your table and capable of standing securely.
3. **Pose:** A seated golem may be easier to assemble than a standing one and still looks impressive.

Tools and Materials

- Stencils or templates for consistent shapes.
- Food-safe structural supports (e.g., wooden skewers or dowels).
- Piping bags with various tips for intricate decorations.
- Edible decorations like candy, frosting, and edible glitter.

Creating the Components

Crafting a large gingerbread golem involves several steps: preparing the dough, shaping the parts, baking, and cooling. Each component must be sturdy and well-supported.

Step 1: The Perfect Dough

Use a stiff gingerbread dough designed for building structures. Refer to *Chapter 1: Building the Foundation* for a detailed recipe. Add an extra ½ cup of flour for additional strength if needed.

Step 2: Shaping and Cutting

1. **Templates:** Draw templates for the golem's body parts (e.g., torso, arms, legs, and head). Use cardboard for durability.
2. **Roll and Cut:** Roll the dough to a uniform thickness of about ¼ inch. Use your templates to cut the shapes.

Step 3: Baking and Cooling

1. **Bake Evenly:** Bake each piece on a flat, parchment-lined baking sheet. For large pieces, bake on low heat (325°F/160°C) for a longer time to prevent uneven cooking.
2. **Cool Completely:** Allow pieces to cool fully before assembly to avoid warping or cracking.

Assembling the Golem

Building a gingerbread golem requires patience and attention to detail. A sturdy adhesive and strategic assembly are crucial for success.

Step 1: Prepare the Adhesive

Use a thick royal icing as "cement" to hold the pieces together. For extra strength, consider melting sugar to create caramel "glue." Be cautious, as melted sugar is extremely hot.

Step 2: Assemble the Base

1. **Start with the Torso:** Assemble the torso and allow it to set fully before attaching limbs or additional parts.
2. **Add Supports:** Use skewers, dowels, or hidden candy canes inside larger pieces for added stability.

Step 3: Attach Limbs and Head

1. Pipe royal icing generously along the edges of each limb and press them into place.
2. Hold each piece steady for a few minutes to ensure a secure bond.
3. Add the head last, using additional supports if necessary.

Step 4: Let It Set

Allow the entire structure to dry for several hours or overnight before decorating.

Decorating Your Gingerbread Golem

The decoration is where your golem comes to life, transforming from a sturdy construction to a magical masterpiece.

Royal Icing Details

1. **Runic Patterns:** Use fine piping tips to draw runes or magical symbols on the golem's surface.
2. **Textural Details:** Create texture on the body with piped designs like fur, armor, or fabric.

Candy and Edible Embellishments

1. **Eyes and Features:** Use gumdrops, jelly beans, or small candies for eyes and facial features.
2. **Armor and Accessories:** Use fondant to craft shields, helmets, or ornaments.
3. **Jewels and Glitz:** Add edible glitter, sugar pearls, or metallic dragees for a regal touch.

Finishing Touches

- Dust with powdered sugar to mimic snow.
- Add LED lights or tea lights to create a glowing, magical effect around your centerpiece.

Enhancing the Presentation

A gingerbread golem is more than its construction; the way it's displayed adds to its impact.

Base and Setting

1. **Edible Base:** Position the golem on an edible base, like a large cookie "platter" decorated with frosting and candy.
2. **Seasonal Accents:** Surround the golem with seasonal elements like mini gingerbread trees, sugar snowflakes, or candy presents.

Interactive Elements

1. **Miniature Golems:** Add smaller, edible golem companions crafted using the techniques in *Chapter 5: Golem Guardians*.
2. **Ritualistic Cookies:** Place symbolic cookies from *Chapter 6: Sweet Rituals* around the golem as offerings or decorations.

Troubleshooting Common Issues

- **Cracked Pieces:** Repair cracks with royal icing or melted sugar and allow them to dry before assembly.
- **Collapsing Structure:** Ensure each section is fully set before adding additional pieces. Use internal supports liberally.
- **Uneven Assembly:** Use a level surface and adjust pieces as needed before the icing sets.

Incorporating Magic and Tradition

To infuse your centerpiece with symbolic meaning, consider the following:

1. **Set an Intention:** Focus on the energy or purpose you want your golem to represent—protection, abundance, or celebration.
2. **Incorporate Personal Touches:** Add initials, symbols, or decorations that reflect your family or community's traditions.
3. **Use Ritualistic Elements:** Decorate with cookies, runes, or offerings that enhance the golem's magical presence.

Conclusion

A gingerbread golem centerpiece is more than an edible creation—it's a labor of love, a symbol of the season's magic, and a testament to your creativity. By carefully planning, constructing, and decorating your golem, you'll create a showstopper confection that becomes the heart of your holiday celebrations. Whether it's a traditional protector, a whimsical companion, or a mythical being, your gingerbread golem will inspire awe and joy for everyone at your table.

Chapter 10: Sweet Defense – Gingerbread Fortifications

In the world of magical golems, fortifications play a central role in symbolizing protection, strength, and resilience. Whether serving as the walls of a mythical kingdom or the stronghold of your Gingerbread Golem centerpiece, these edible fortresses are as functional as they are fantastical. This chapter will guide you through the process of designing, baking, and constructing intricate gingerbread walls and fortresses, turning your table into a magical battlefield or enchanted castle.

The Mythical Significance of Fortifications

Fortifications have been integral to tales of magic and mythology. Walls and castles symbolize security, strength, and the power to withstand external threats. In the context of gingerbread creations, these edible structures become a playful and symbolic representation of protection—both physical and spiritual. By crafting a gingerbread fortress, you're not just baking; you're weaving a story of defense and unity.

Planning Your Edible Fortress

A successful gingerbread fortress begins with careful planning. From the size and design to the details of its construction, each element should reflect the theme and story of your creation.

Step 1: Choose Your Design

Decide on the type of fortification you want to create:

- **Castle:** Towers, drawbridges, and crenellated walls for a regal appearance.
- **Fortress Wall:** A sturdy perimeter with gates and battlements.
- **Magical Stronghold:** Whimsical shapes, glowing elements, and runes etched into the walls.

Step 2: Scale and Dimensions

Determine the size of your structure based on the space available on your table and the materials you'll need.

- Use graph paper to sketch a scaled plan of your fortress, including measurements for walls, towers, and decorative elements.

Step 3: Templates

Create sturdy templates from cardboard for all major components, such as walls, doors, windows, and towers. These ensure consistent shapes during cutting and assembly.

The Perfect Dough for Fortifications

For large-scale structures, your gingerbread dough must be sturdy and resistant to warping. Use the structural dough recipe from *Chapter 1: Building the Foundation*, adding ½ cup of flour for extra rigidity if needed.

Rolling and Cutting

- Roll the dough to a uniform thickness of ¼ **inch** for walls and structural elements.
- Cut shapes using your templates and transfer them to a baking sheet lined with parchment paper.

Baking Tips for Structural Pieces

1. **Bake at Low Heat:** Use a lower oven temperature (325°F/ 160°C) to ensure even baking and reduce the risk of burning large pieces.
2. **Reinforce Edges:** Trim the edges of the dough while it's still warm to ensure clean, straight lines.
3. **Cool Completely:** Allow all pieces to cool on a flat surface to prevent bending or warping.

Building Your Fortress

Assembling a gingerbread fortress requires patience and a strong adhesive. Here's how to create a solid structure:

Step 1: Prepare the Adhesive

- Use royal icing as your main adhesive. Its thick consistency sets quickly and creates a firm bond.
- For extra strength, use melted sugar as "caramel glue," but handle with care—it's extremely hot.

Step 2: Construct the Walls

1. **Base Layer:** Start with a sturdy base, such as a large cookie sheet or a board covered in parchment paper.
2. **Attach Walls:** Pipe a thick line of icing along the edges of the wall pieces and press them together. Hold each piece in place for a few minutes to allow the icing to set.
3. **Support the Walls:** Use cans or jars to hold the walls upright while the icing dries.

Step 3: Add Towers and Decorative Features

- Attach cylindrical pieces, such as prebaked cookie tubes or cut gingerbread rounds, to create towers.
- Use smaller cookie pieces to add crenellations, gates, and other architectural details.

Step 4: Let It Set

Allow the entire structure to dry overnight before adding heavy decorations or accessories.

Decorating Your Fortress

Bring your fortress to life with intricate decorations and edible embellishments.

Royal Icing Details

- Pipe runes, symbols, or decorative patterns onto the walls.
- Use icing to create vines, cracks, or aged textures for a weathered effect.

Candy and Edible Accents

1. **Windows and Doors:** Use square or rectangular candies for windows and chocolate bars for doors.
2. **Turrets and Battlements:** Add small sugar cubes or gumdrops to create crenellations along the tops of walls.
3. **Pathways and Courtyards:** Crush graham crackers to mimic sand or stone for pathways inside the fortress.

Glowing Elements

Add LED tea lights or fairy lights inside the fortress for a magical, glowing effect.

Enhancing the Story

Every gingerbread fortress tells a story. Use these ideas to add depth and meaning to your creation:

Incorporate a Theme

- **Seasonal Magic:** Use snow-like frosting and winter-themed decorations to reflect the season.
- **Battle-Ready Stronghold:** Include miniature golems (from *Chapter 5*) as guards on the walls.
- **Mythical Citadel:** Add elements like sugar glass "windows" or candy "jewels" to create an enchanted feel.

Symbolic Elements

- **Runes and Sigils:** Etch protective runes into the walls for a mythical touch.
- **Offerings:** Surround the fortress with cookies or truffles as symbolic offerings (see *Chapter 6*).

Recipe for Edible Brick Accents
Ingredients:

- 2 cups granulated sugar
- ½ cup water
- Food coloring (optional)

Instructions:

1. Heat the sugar and water in a saucepan over medium heat until the sugar dissolves and begins to boil.
2. Cook without stirring until the mixture reaches 300°F (hard crack stage).
3. Pour onto a lined baking sheet and allow to cool.
4. Break into pieces to mimic bricks or stones and attach to your fortress with royal icing.

Troubleshooting Common Issues

- **Warped Walls:** Trim the edges of baked pieces while warm and cool them flat.
- **Cracked Pieces:** Reinforce cracked pieces with royal icing or melted sugar.
- **Weak Structure:** Use internal supports like skewers or dowels to stabilize larger sections.

Interactive Features

Make your fortress a centerpiece that engages your guests:

1. **Breakable Walls:** Design sections that can be "broken" to reveal hidden treats or surprises.
2. **Edible Gates:** Create a functioning gate using licorice ropes or pretzel sticks.
3. **Miniature Figures:** Add edible characters, like gingerbread knights or golems, to guard the fortress.

Conclusion

A gingerbread fortress is more than an edible creation—it's an artistic expression of protection and celebration. By combining sturdy construction, creative decorations, and a touch of storytelling, you can craft a centerpiece that captivates your guests and elevates your holiday table. Whether it's a regal castle, a mythical stronghold, or a whimsical wall of defense, your gingerbread fortifications will stand as a testament to the magic and wonder of the season.

Chapter 11: Darkly Sweet – Gothic Gingerbread Delights

While gingerbread is often associated with warm, festive cheer, it also has a darker, more mysterious side waiting to be explored. Gothic gingerbread creations are rich, dramatic, and full of deep flavors, blending the sweetness of tradition with the haunting allure of the macabre. In this chapter, we'll delve into recipes that use black cocoa, burnt sugar, and other bold ingredients to craft sophisticated and striking desserts that are as visually captivating as they are delicious.

The Allure of Gothic Gingerbread

Gothic gingerbread celebrates contrasts: light and shadow, sweet and bitter, ornate and raw. These recipes embrace deep, intense flavors and dramatic presentations, perfect for holiday tables that dare to be different. Inspired by the Victorian Gothic aesthetic, these treats also carry the richness of centuries-old culinary traditions.

Key Ingredients for Gothic Gingerbread

To achieve the distinctive flavors and aesthetics of Gothic-inspired desserts, consider these ingredients:

1. **Black Cocoa Powder:** This ultra-dark cocoa powder delivers a deep, bittersweet flavor and a striking black hue.
2. **Burnt Sugar (Caramel):** Adds complexity with smoky, bitter notes that balance sweetness.
3. **Molasses:** A key ingredient in traditional gingerbread, its bold flavor is amplified in Gothic recipes.
4. **Espresso Powder:** Enhances the chocolatey depth of black cocoa and complements the spices.
5. **Dark Spices:** Star anise, allspice, and cardamom bring exotic, mysterious flavors.
6. **Decorative Elements:** Edible silver or gold leaf, metallic dragees, and dark-colored candies create an elegant, otherworldly appearance.

Recipe 1: Black Cocoa Gingerbread Cookies
Ingredients:

- 2 ½ cups all-purpose flour
- ½ cup black cocoa powder
- 1 teaspoon baking soda
- 1 teaspoon ground cinnamon
- ½ teaspoon ground ginger
- ¼ teaspoon ground cloves
- ½ teaspoon salt
- ½ cup unsalted butter, softened
- ½ cup dark brown sugar
- ½ cup molasses
- 1 large egg

Instructions:

1. **Prepare the Dough:** In a medium bowl, whisk together flour, black cocoa powder, baking soda, spices, and salt. In a large bowl, cream the butter and brown sugar until light and fluffy. Add molasses and egg, mixing until combined. Gradually incorporate the dry ingredients.
2. **Chill the Dough:** Divide the dough into two disks, wrap in plastic wrap, and refrigerate for at least 2 hours.
3. **Roll and Cut:** Preheat oven to 350°F (175°C). Roll the dough to ¼-inch thickness and cut into gothic-inspired shapes (bats, moons, or ornate patterns).
4. **Bake:** Place on a parchment-lined baking sheet and bake for 8–10 minutes. Let cool completely before decorating.

Decoration Tips:

- Pipe with royal icing tinted black, silver, or deep red.
- Add metallic dragees for a dramatic touch.

Recipe 2: Burnt Sugar Gingerbread Tartlets
Ingredients for Burnt Sugar Filling:

- 1 cup granulated sugar
- ½ cup heavy cream
- 2 tablespoons unsalted butter
- ½ teaspoon sea salt

Ingredients for Tart Shells:

- 1 ½ cups all-purpose flour
- ½ cup unsalted butter, chilled and cubed
- ¼ cup powdered sugar
- 1 egg yolk
- 1 tablespoon black cocoa powder
- 1 teaspoon gingerbread spice blend

Instructions:

1. **Make the Burnt Sugar Filling:** In a heavy saucepan, melt sugar over medium heat, swirling the pan to ensure even caramelization. Once amber-colored, remove from heat and carefully stir in cream, butter, and salt. Allow to cool.
2. **Prepare Tart Dough:** Combine flour, black cocoa, powdered sugar, and spice blend. Cut in butter until the mixture resembles

coarse crumbs. Add egg yolk and mix until a dough forms. Chill for 30 minutes.

3. **Assemble Tartlets:** Roll out dough and press into tartlet pans. Bake at 350°F (175°C) for 12–15 minutes. Cool completely before filling with burnt sugar caramel.

4. **Decorate:** Garnish with edible gold leaf or a sprinkle of black sea salt.

Recipe 3: Gothic Gingerbread Cake with Molasses Glaze
Ingredients for Cake:

- 2 cups all-purpose flour
- ½ cup black cocoa powder
- 1 teaspoon baking soda
- 1 teaspoon ground cinnamon
- ½ teaspoon ground star anise
- ½ teaspoon ground cardamom
- ¼ teaspoon salt
- 1 cup molasses
- ½ cup dark brown sugar
- 1 cup hot coffee
- ½ cup vegetable oil
- 2 large eggs

Ingredients for Glaze:

- ½ cup molasses
- 1 cup powdered sugar
- 1–2 tablespoons milk

Instructions:

1. **Prepare the Batter:** In a large bowl, whisk together dry ingredients (flour, cocoa, baking soda, spices, salt). In another bowl, combine molasses, brown sugar, hot coffee, oil, and eggs. Gradually add wet ingredients to dry, mixing until smooth.
2. **Bake the Cake:** Preheat oven to 350°F (175°C). Pour batter into a greased and floured Bundt pan. Bake for 40–45 minutes or until a toothpick inserted in the center comes out clean. Cool completely.

3. **Make the Glaze:** Whisk together molasses, powdered sugar, and milk until smooth. Drizzle over the cooled cake.
4. **Decorate:** Add edible glitter, black sugar crystals, or candied ginger for a gothic flourish.

Recipe 4: Midnight Gingerbread Truffles
Ingredients:

- 2 cups crushed gingersnap cookies
- ½ cup black cocoa powder
- 4 ounces cream cheese, softened
- 2 tablespoons molasses
- 1 teaspoon espresso powder
- 8 ounces dark chocolate, melted

Instructions:

1. **Mix the Base:** Combine crushed gingersnaps, black cocoa, cream cheese, molasses, and espresso powder. Mix until a dough forms.
2. **Shape Truffles:** Roll into small balls and chill for 20 minutes.
3. **Coat in Chocolate:** Dip truffles into melted dark chocolate and place on parchment paper. Let set completely.
4. **Decorate:** Dust with cocoa powder or drizzle with red-tinted chocolate for a dramatic effect.

Decorative Techniques for Gothic Gingerbread

1. **Use Dark Colors:** Incorporate black, deep red, or metallic shades for a striking visual impact.
2. **Add Edible Gothic Accents:** Use edible skulls, crosses, or bats as decorations.
3. **Incorporate Textures:** Create cracks, swirls, or cobweb effects with piped royal icing.

Pairing Gothic Gingerbread with Drinks

Serve these rich creations with complementary beverages for a fully immersive experience:

- **Spiced Mulled Wine:** Adds warmth and complements the spices.
- **Espresso or Coffee:** Enhances the bittersweet flavors of black cocoa.
- **Dark Hot Chocolate:** A velvety, indulgent pairing for truffles or cakes.

Troubleshooting Common Issues

- **Bitter Flavors:** Balance the boldness of black cocoa or burnt sugar with sweeteners like molasses or brown sugar.
- **Dry Textures:** Add moisture with molasses or oil to prevent overly dry baked goods.
- **Fading Colors:** Use gel or powder food coloring to maintain intense hues.

Conclusion

Gothic gingerbread delights are an artistic and flavorful twist on traditional holiday treats. These dark, decadent recipes combine bold flavors, dramatic aesthetics, and a touch of the mysterious to create desserts that are both hauntingly beautiful and irresistibly delicious. Whether you're crafting cookies, cakes, or truffles, your Gothic-inspired creations will bring an air of elegance and enchantment to any gathering.

Chapter 12: The Final Awakening – Edible Charms and Incantations

In the realm of magical baking, the final touches often carry the most profound meaning. Edible charms, sigils, and infused decorations elevate your gingerbread creations from culinary delights to vessels of intention and enchantment. In this chapter, we'll explore how to imbue your gingerbread treats with deeper significance through the incorporation of sugar sigils, enchanted symbols, and intention-infused decorations. By crafting these edible charms and combining them with simple incantations, you can awaken the magical potential of your creations, turning them into powerful tools for manifestation, celebration, and connection.

The Magic of Edible Charms

Edible charms combine the sensory pleasure of food with the symbolic power of intention. These elements work together to create desserts that not only nourish the body but also align with spiritual or emotional goals. From protective sugar sigils to blessings etched into royal icing, these techniques invite you to infuse your gingerbread golems, fortresses, or Gothic treats with purposeful energy.

Crafting Sugar Sigils

Sigils are magical symbols created to focus intent or energy. Incorporating them into your gingerbread designs enhances their spiritual significance.

How to Create a Sigil:

1. **State Your Intention:** Write a simple, positive phrase, such as "Protection for All" or "Joyful Celebrations."
2. **Simplify the Phrase:** Remove repeating letters and reduce the remaining ones to their basic shapes.
3. **Combine the Letters:** Rearrange and stylize the shapes into a unique, symbolic design.
4. **Finalize the Sigil:** Refine the design into a cohesive symbol.

Incorporating Sugar Sigils:

1. **Icing Designs:** Pipe the sigil onto your gingerbread with royal icing. Use contrasting colors for visibility.
2. **Carved Patterns:** Etch the sigil into uncooked dough before baking. The heat will "seal" the intention into the piece.
3. **Candy Embellishments:** Create sigils using crushed candy or edible glitter arranged on the surface of cookies or cakes.

Edible Decorations Infused with Intention

Adding infused elements to your decorations allows you to embed specific energies into your creations.

Blessed Spices and Sugars

1. **Herbal Sugars:** Mix sugar with ground herbs like lavender (for peace), rosemary (for protection), or mint (for abundance). Let the mixture infuse overnight before using it as a decorative dusting or glaze base.
2. **Spice Sprinkles:** Blend cinnamon, nutmeg, and a pinch of star anise to create a protective spice mix. Sprinkle onto frosting or glaze.

Crystals and Gems (Edible Versions):

1. **Sugar Crystals:** Use rock candy or colored sugar to mimic gemstones. Assign meanings to each color (e.g., red for love, green for prosperity).
2. **Isomalt Creations:** Melt isomalt to craft edible "crystals" shaped like amulets or pendants.

Runic and Symbolic Decorations:

1. Pipe or carve runes representing health, wealth, or protection into your gingerbread designs.
2. Use metallic edible paints to highlight runic patterns for a dramatic effect.

Enchantment Rituals for Baking

Infuse your baking process with intention by incorporating simple rituals.

Setting the Space:

1. Clean your workspace and light a candle or incense to focus your energy.
2. Play music or create silence to foster concentration.

Blessing the Ingredients:

1. Hold your hands over each ingredient and focus on its purpose in the recipe. For example:
   ◦ Sugar for sweetness and joy.
   ◦ Spices for warmth and protection.
2. Speak an affirmation or incantation as you blend the ingredients.

Stirring with Intention:

1. Stir clockwise to bring energy in (e.g., abundance or joy).
2. Stir counterclockwise to release energy (e.g., negativity or fear).

Recipes with Edible Charms and Incantations
Recipe 1: Protection Sigil Gingerbread Shields
Ingredients:

- Sturdy gingerbread dough (see *Chapter 1*)
- Royal icing (thick consistency)
- Edible glitter or gold dust

Instructions:

1. **Cut the Shields:** Use a shield-shaped cutter or carve the shape freehand from rolled dough.
2. **Bake and Cool:** Bake until firm and allow to cool completely.
3. **Add Sigils:** Pipe protection sigils onto the shields with royal icing. Once dry, dust with edible glitter or gold dust.
4. **Activate the Charms:** Hold the shields and recite a protection incantation, such as:
   "By sugar and spice, this charm I weave,
   To guard and protect, this I believe."

Recipe 2: Joyful Celebration Cookies
Ingredients:

- Gingerbread cookie dough
- Infused sugar (see above)
- Colored royal icing

Instructions:

1. **Prepare the Dough:** Roll and cut the dough into festive shapes (stars, hearts, etc.).
2. **Etch Words:** Use a toothpick to carve words like "Joy," "Love," or "Harmony" into the dough before baking.
3. **Bake and Decorate:** Once baked, pipe icing along the edges and sprinkle with infused sugar.
4. **Bless the Cookies:** Arrange the cookies on a platter and recite:
   "May these cookies bring joy and cheer,
   To all who taste them, far and near."

Recipe 3: Empowering Golem Medallions
Ingredients:

- Gingerbread dough
- Black cocoa icing or edible paint
- Edible gems or sugar crystals

Instructions:

1. **Create Medallions:** Cut large circles from the dough to represent medallions or amulets.
2. **Add Sigils:** Etch empowering sigils into the dough before baking.
3. **Decorate:** Highlight the sigils with black cocoa icing or metallic edible paint. Place sugar crystals in the center as a "power stone."
4. **Ritual Activation:** Hold the medallions and chant:
   "Strength and courage, power and might,
   In this charm, I seal the light."

Using Edible Charms
Once your edible charms are ready, share them with intention:

1. **Gift Giving:** Present the treats as thoughtful, magical gifts, explaining their significance.
2. **Festive Displays:** Incorporate them into your holiday decor as edible centerpieces.
3. **Personal Rituals:** Eat a charm mindfully while focusing on its intention, or share with loved ones during a meaningful gathering.

Troubleshooting Charm Crafting

- **Smudged Sigils:** Allow each layer of icing or decoration to dry fully before adding more details.
- **Unclear Etchings:** Press firmly into the dough with a skewer or knife to ensure designs remain visible after baking.
- **Flavors Too Intense:** Balance strong herbal or spice infusions with sweet elements like honey or vanilla.

Conclusion

Edible charms and incantations transform your gingerbread creations into more than just desserts—they become tools of intention and connection. By combining thoughtful designs, infused ingredients, and simple rituals, you can craft treats that inspire wonder and elevate the holiday season. Whether you're baking for celebration, protection, or simple joy, these enchanted recipes ensure that every bite carries a touch of magic.

Appendix: Golem Baker's Tools and Techniques

Creating intricate and showstopping gingerbread golems requires the right tools, mastery of techniques, and a plan for addressing challenges. This appendix provides a comprehensive guide to the essential tools, advanced methods, and troubleshooting tips to ensure your gingerbread creations are successful and enchanting.

Essential Tools for the Golem Baker

1. Measuring Tools

- **Measuring Cups and Spoons:** Accurate measurements are crucial for balancing dough consistency, spice blends, and icing.
- **Kitchen Scale:** For precise weight measurements, especially when scaling recipes.

2. Mixing and Shaping Tools

- **Stand Mixer or Hand Mixer:** Perfect for creaming butter and sugar, mixing dough, and whipping royal icing.
- **Mixing Bowls:** Multiple bowls of various sizes are essential for separating ingredients and mixing colors.
- **Rolling Pins:** A nonstick or marble rolling pin ensures even dough thickness. Adjustable rings are ideal for maintaining uniformity.
- **Spatulas and Scrapers:** Silicone spatulas for scraping bowls and dough scrapers for handling sticky or crumbly dough.

3. Cutting and Shaping Tools

- **Cookie Cutters:** Shapes ranging from basic circles to intricate designs for golem parts and accents.
- **Knives and Blades:** Sharp paring knives or X-Acto blades for detailed cuts and custom shapes.
- **Templates:** Cardboard or plastic templates help maintain consistency in large or intricate pieces.

4. Baking Essentials

- **Parchment Paper or Silicone Mats:** Prevent sticking and ensure even baking.
- **Baking Sheets:** Sturdy sheets with no warping under high heat for perfectly flat gingerbread.
- **Cooling Racks:** Allow airflow for even cooling and prevent soggy bottoms.

5. Decorating Tools

- **Piping Bags and Tips:** Essential for precision icing work. Use various tips for detailing, flooding, and writing.
- **Fondant Tools:** For sculpting and shaping edible decorations like accessories or runic accents.
- **Food-Safe Brushes:** For applying edible paints, luster dust, or glitter.
- **Edible Markers:** For fine details and writing on dry royal icing.

6. Structural Tools

- **Skewers and Dowels:** Provide internal support for large pieces or standing structures.
- **Edible Glue (Royal Icing or Melted Sugar):** Ensures a strong bond between pieces.

7. Advanced Tools

- **Isomalt Kit:** For crafting edible windows, jewels, or decorative accents.
- **Airbrush Kit:** For adding gradients and fine details with edible colors.
- **Clay Modeling Tools:** Useful for shaping intricate fondant or dough designs.

Advanced Techniques for Gingerbread Mastery

1. Dough Management

- **Chilling Dough:** Always chill dough before rolling to ensure easier handling and precise cuts.
- **Layering Flavors:** Infuse spices overnight for a deeper flavor profile. Add a touch of espresso powder or black cocoa for boldness in advanced recipes.

2. Shaping and Cutting

- **Uniform Thickness:** Roll dough between two guide sticks or an adjustable rolling pin for consistent thickness, especially for structural pieces.
- **Sharp Edges:** Use a straight-edge ruler or a sharp blade to trim edges immediately after baking while the dough is still warm.

3. Baking Techniques

- **Low and Slow:** Bake larger or thicker pieces at a lower temperature for longer to prevent overbrowning.
- **Drying in the Oven:** After baking, turn off the oven and let pieces sit inside for 10–15 minutes to ensure complete dryness.

4. Assembly Tricks

- **Anchor Points:** Always assemble from the base up, allowing each section to dry fully before adding more weight.
- **Double Adhesive Layers:** Use both royal icing and melted sugar for maximum strength in large constructions.

- **Support Structures:** Use temporary supports like cans or jars during the drying process.

5. Decoration Mastery

- **Icing Consistency:** Adjust icing thickness depending on its use: stiff for structural work, medium for piping, and thin for flooding.
- **Color Blending:** Mix gel food coloring for rich, custom hues. Layer edible paints for dimensional effects.
- **Texturing:** Use piping tips or fondant tools to create textures like fur, armor, or woodgrain.

Troubleshooting Tips
Structural Issues

- **Cracking Pieces:** Avoid overmixing dough, which creates air pockets. Repair cracks with royal icing or melted sugar.
- **Collapsing Structures:** Ensure each section is fully set before adding more. Reinforce weak areas with dowels or extra icing.
- **Warping:** Roll dough evenly and chill thoroughly before cutting. Trim edges after baking for straight lines.

Icing Problems

- **Runny Icing:** Add powdered sugar to thicken; ensure you're beating it long enough to hold stiff peaks.
- **Air Bubbles:** Pop bubbles in flooded icing with a toothpick or tap the surface gently before it sets.
- **Bleeding Colors:** Allow each layer to dry completely before adding new colors. Use gel colors for minimal bleeding.

Flavor or Texture Issues

- **Bitter Taste:** Over-baking or too much molasses can cause bitterness. Adjust baking time and ingredient ratios.
- **Soft Structures:** Ensure pieces are fully baked and dry before assembly. Store in a cool, dry place to prevent softening.

Tips for Working with Large and Complex Golem Creations

1. **Break It Into Sections:** Assemble towers, walls, or golem limbs separately before combining them.
2. **Use Templates:** Plan and cut all pieces in advance to ensure proper alignment during assembly.
3. **Plan for Transport:** If the centerpiece needs to move, use a sturdy, flat base like a baking tray or cake board. Secure the golem with royal icing to the base.

Storage and Preservation

1. **Storage:** Keep baked pieces in airtight containers to preserve freshness until assembly.
2. **Finished Pieces:** Store completed structures in a cool, dry place to prevent icing from melting or softening.
3. **Long-Term Display:** Spray finished pieces with a food-safe sealant for display purposes, making them inedible but preserved.

Making the Process Magical

Incorporating intention and joy into your baking process can elevate your creations.

- **Set Your Intention:** Before beginning, focus on what your gingerbread creation represents (e.g., protection, abundance, celebration).
- **Work in a Sacred Space:** Create a clean, organized workspace with calming music or scents to enhance your focus.

Conclusion

The art of crafting gingerbread golems and confections is as much about the tools and techniques as it is about creativity and intention. With the guidance provided in this appendix, you'll have everything you need to perfect your recipes, overcome challenges, and create edible masterpieces that captivate and inspire. Whether you're building a simple figure or an elaborate fortress, these tips and tools ensure that your gingerbread creations are as magical as they are memorable.

<u>Message from the Author:</u>

I hope you enjoyed this book, I love astrology and knew there was not a book such as this out on the shelf. I love metaphysical items as well. Please check out my other books:

-Life of Government Benefits

-My life of Hell

-My life with Hydrocephalus

-Red Sky

-World Domination:Woman's rule

-World Domination:Woman's Rule 2: The War

-Life and Banishment of Apophis: book 1

-The Kidney Friendly Diet

-The Ultimate Hemp Cookbook

-Creating a Dispensary(legally)

-Cleanliness throughout life: the importance of showering from childhood to adulthood.

-Strong Roots: The Risks of Overcoddling children

-Hemp Horoscopes: Cosmic Insights and Earthly Healing

- Celestial Hemp Navigating the Zodiac: Through the Green Cosmos

-Astrological Hemp: Aligning The Stars with Earth's Ancient Herb

-The Astrological Guide to Hemp: Stars, Signs, and Sacred Leaves

-Green Growth: Innovative Marketing Strategies for your Hemp Products and Dispensary

-Cosmic Cannabis

-Astrological Munchies

-Henry The Hemp

-Zodiacal Roots: The Astrological Soul Of Hemp

- Green Constellations: Intersection of Hemp and Zodiac

-Hemp in The Houses: An astrological Adventure Through The Cannabis Galaxy

-Galactic Ganja Guide

Heavenly Hemp

Zodiac Leaves

Doctor Who Astrology

Cannastrology

Stellar Satvias and Cosmic Indicas

Celestial Cannabis: A Zodiac Journey

AstroHerbology: The Sky and The Soil: Volume 1

AstroHerbology:Celestial Cannabis:Volume 2

Cosmic Cannabis Cultivation

The Starry Guide to Herbal Harmony: Volume 1

The Starry Guide to Herbal Harmony: Cannabis Universe: Volume 2

Yugioh Astrology: Astrological Guide to Deck, Duels and more

Nightmare Mansion: Echoes of The Abyss

Nightmare Mansion 2: Legacy of Shadows

Nightmare Mansion 3: Shadows of the Forgotten

Nightmare Mansion 4: Echoes of the Damned

The Life and Banishment of Apophis: Book 2

Nightmare Mansion: Halls of Despair

Healing with Herb: Cannabis and Hydrocephalus

Planetary Pot: Aligning with Astrological Herbs: Volume 1

Fast Track to Freedom: 30 Days to Financial Independence Using AI, Assets, and Agile Hustles

Cosmic Hemp Pathways

How to Become Financially Free in 30 Days: 10,000 Paths to Prosperity

Zodiacal Herbage: Astrological Insights: Volume 1

Nightmare Mansion: Whispers in the Walls

The Daleks Invade Atlantis
Henry the hemp and Hydrocephalus

10X The Kidney Friendly Diet
Cannabis Universe: Adult coloring book
Hemp Astrology: The Healing Power of the Stars
Zodiacal Herbage: Astrological Insights: Cannabis Universe: Volume 2
<u>Planetary Pot: Aligning with Astrological Herbs: Cannabis Universes: Volume 2</u>
Doctor Who Meets the Replicators and SG-1: The Ultimate Battle for Survival
Nightmare Mansion: Curse of the Blood Moon
<u>The Celestial Stoner: A Guide to the Zodiac</u>
Cosmic Pleasures: Sex Toy Astrology for Every Sign
Hydrocephalus Astrology: Navigating the Stars and Healing Waters
Lapis and the Mischievous Chocolate Bar

Celestial Positions: Sexual Astrology for Every Sign
Apophis's Shadow Work Journal: : A Journey of Self-Discovery and Healing
Kinky Cosmos: Sexual Kink Astrology for Every Sign
Digital Cosmos: The Astrological Digimon Compendium
Stellar Seeds: The Cosmic Guide to Growing with Astrology
Apophis's Daily Gratitude Journal

Cat Astrology: Feline Mysteries of the Cosmos
The Cosmic Kama Sutra: An Astrological Guide to Sexual Positions
Unleash Your Potential: A Guided Journal Powered by AI Insights
Whispers of the Enchanted Grove

Cosmic Pleasures: An Astrological Guide to Sexual Kinks

369, 12 Manifestation Journal

Whisper of the nocturne journal(blank journal for writing or drawing)

The Boogey Book

Locked In Reflection: A Chastity Journey Through Locktober

Generating Wealth Quickly:

How to Generate $100,000 in 24 Hours

Star Magic: Harness the Power of the Universe

The Flatulence Chronicles: A Fart Journal for Self-Discovery

The Doctor and The Death Moth

Seize the Day: A Personal Seizure Tracking Journal

The Ultimate Boogeyman Safari: A Journey into the Boogie World and Beyond

Whispers of Samhain: 1,000 Spells of Love, Luck, and Lunar Magic: Samhain Spell Book

Apophis's guides:

Witch's Spellbook Crafting Guide for Halloween

<u>Frost & Flame: The Enchanted Yule Grimoire of 1000 Winter Spells</u>

<u>The Ultimate Boogey Goo Guide & Spooky Activities for Halloween Fun</u>

Harmony of the Scales: A Libra's Spellcraft for Balance and Beauty

The Enchanted Advent: 36 Days of Christmas Wonders

Nightmare Mansion: The Labyrinth of Screams

Harvest of Enchantment: 1,000 Spells of Gratitude, Love, and Fortune for Thanksgiving

The Boogey Chronicles: A Journal of Nightly Encounters and Shadowy Secrets

The 12 Days of Financial Freedom: A Step-by-Step Christmas Countdown to Transform Your Finances

Sigil of the Eternal Spiral Blank Journal

A Christmas Feast: Timeless Recipes for Every Meal

Holiday Stress-Free Solutions: A Survival Guide to Thriving During the Festive Season

Yu-Gi-Oh! Holiday Gifting Mastery: The Ultimate Guide for Fans and Newcomers Alike

Holiday Harmony: A Hydrocephalus Survival Guide for the Festive Season

Celestial Craft: The Witch's Almanac for 2025 – A Cosmic Guide to Manifestations, Moons, and Mystical Events

Doctor Who: The Toymaker's Winter Wonderland

Tulsa King Unveiled: A Thrilling Guide to Stallone's Mafia Masterpiece

Pendulum Craft: A Complete Guide to Crafting and Using Personalized Divination Tools

Nightmare Mansion: Santa's Eternal Eve

Starlight Noel: A Cosmic Journey through Christmas Mysteries

The Dark Architect: Unlocking the Blueprint of Existence

Surviving the Embrace: The Ultimate Guide to Encounters with The Hugging Molly

The Enchanted Codex: Secrets of the Craft for Witches, Wiccans, and Pagans

Harvest of Gratitude: A Complete Thanksgiving Guide

Yuletide Essentials: A Complete Guide to an Authentic and Magical Christmas

Celestial Smokes: A Cosmic Guide to Cigars and Astrology

Living in Balance: A Comprehensive Survival Guide to Thriving with Diabetes Insipidus

Cosmic Symbiosis: The Venom Zodiac Chronicles

The Cursed Paw of Ambition

Cosmic Symbiosis: The Astrological Venom Journal

Celestial Wonders Unfold: A Stargazer's Guide to the Cosmos (2024-2029)

The Ultimate Black Friday Prepper's Guide: Mastering Shopping Strategies and Savings

Cosmic Sales: The Astrological Guide to Black Friday Shopping

Legends of the Corn Mother and Other Harvest Myths

Whispers of the Harvest: The Corn Mother's Journal

The Evergreen Spellbook

The Doctor Meets the Boogeyman

The White Witch of Rose Hall's SpellBook

The Gingerbread Golem's Shadow: A Study in Sweet Darkness

The Gingerbread Golem Codex: An Academic Exploration of Sweet Myths

The Gingerbread Golem Grimoire: Sweet Magicks and Spells for the Festive Witch

The Curse of the Gingerbread Golem

10-minute Christmas Crafts for kids

Christmas Crisis Solutions: The Ultimate Last-Minute Survival Guide

Gingerbread Golem Recipes: Holiday Treats with a Magical Twist

The Infinite Key: Unlocking Mystical Secrets of the Ages

Enchanted Yule: A Wiccan and Pagan Guide to a Magical and Memorable Season

Dinosaurs of Power: Unlocking Ancient Magick

Astro-Dinos: The Cosmic Guide to Prehistoric Wisdom

Gallifrey's Yule Logs: A Festive Doctor Who Cookbook

The Dino Grimoire: Secrets of Prehistoric Magick

The Gift They Never Knew They Needed

If you want solar for your home go here: https://www.harborsolar.live/apophisenterprises/

Get Some Tarot cards: https://www.makeplayingcards.com/sell/apophis-occult-shop

Get some   shirts: https://www.bonfire.com/store/apophis-shirt-emporium/

<u>**Instagrams:**</u>
@apophis_enterprises,
@apophisbookemporium,
@apophisscardshop
Twitter: @apophisenterpr1
Tiktok:@apophisenterprise
Youtube: @sg1fan23477, @FiresideRetreatKingdom
Hive: @sg1fan23477
CheeLee: @SG1fan23477

Podcast: Apophis Chat Zone: https://open.spotify.com/show/5zXbrCLEV2xzCp8ybrfHsk?si=fb4d4fdbdce44dec

Newsletter: https://apophiss-newsletter-27c897.beehiiv.com/